Chasing Rainbows

...will have you pursuing the bag outside the will of God

Copyright

Cover Design: Prymel Elements | www.prymelelements.com
Cover Photography: EJVisualz | ejvisualz316@gmail.com

Paperback ISBN: 978-1-7355461-7-9
Hardcover ISBN: 978-1-7355461-9-3 | 978-1-7355461-8-6
Kindle ASIN: B08L4LMNTL

10 9 8 7 6 5 4 3 2
Printed in the United States

Priceless Publishing
Coral Springs, Fl
www.pricelesspublishing.co

Chasing Rainbows

...makes you unrealistic in going after your goals and dreams.

Contents.

Part 1:

Part 2:

About The Author

Part 1

Disclaimer.

This book is for the imperfect Christ believers, Jesus lovers, and willing-to-learn women and men of God. The stories and lessons shared in this book represent what I have figured out so far on my faith journey. This book is not a victory-to-triumph story, rather it was written to offer guidance to the faith-based entrepreneur or those lost in purpose. Due to my imperfections in following Christ, I can only share what He has instructed me to share, which is faith and business.

Prelude.

Chasing Rainbows means that you are being unrealistic in going after a goal. In other words, you are searching for the pot of gold at the end of the rainbow that was never there to begin with. In fact, when you think about it, growing up, you are typically told that what's on the other side of the rainbow is a pot of gold. It is essentially the land of milk and honey. While desiring the pot of gold and getting to the land of milk and honey is not wrong, it's wrong to make it a priority over God's will.

When I started my business, I was chasing rainbows and it distracted me from God's will. I was unrealistic in trying to go after my business goals without God. I was a believer, I was faith-based, I knew God and His powers, but when it came to my business, I did not include Him. Even though I remember being told by a business colleague not to speak of God too much in my business to avoid being too religious, ultimately this was my choice. It was a very bad choice, and I was even told that sounding too religious could have a negative effect on my business when that was not my target market.

For the longest time, I was torn. I prayed to God about my business, but never spoke of Him publicly to avoid sounding too religious. Besides, I was working with mentors who 'knew' what they were doing. I knew what God called me to do, yet I struggled with speaking about God where I saw fit because I had to 'protect my brand'. See, I was a first-generation college graduate and entrepreneur for my family. And I learned on my college journey that being the first will cost you all the mistakes, especially when there is a lack of family leadership or mentorship to offer guidance.

So when it came to entrepreneurship, I didn't want to make any mistakes as I did on my college journey. All I knew was that I had expertise in particular areas and subject matters, and I was ready to venture off into business. I wanted mentorship and help in other areas of business like legal, financial, and marketing, so I sought after that. I was ready to be the resource my family needed financially. That was my focus – being financially secure so I could help my family. I wanted to build generational wealth. But where was God in my Priceless Plan?

I was chasing rainbows in my business, searching for the 'pot of gold' without God. When in reality I needed God. Perhaps it was never about chasing the rainbows, it was the fact that I was doing it without God. Forgetting that He is God, not just over my life but also my business. When I visualize my life back then, it was almost as if there were homes, cars, businesses, and bags of money on the other side of the rainbow that I was chasing. I was chasing rainbows to get to the business pot of gold.

What's on the other side of your rainbow?

Grab a pen and piece of paper, and give me your best rainbow illustration and your ah-mazing stick-figure sketches of what you're chasing on the other side of it.

Tweet me on Twitter @drsidjaeprice or tag me on Instagram @drsidjaeprice with your work of art.

Too much religion.
Not enough God.

Life.

I was born in Los Angeles, California, at UCLA to be exact. However, I spent most of my life being raised in Kingston, Jamaica. Then I resided in New York for about two years and moved to Florida. I know it's a lot, and I don't know if God will have me go to any other places, but I'm always open. I was never one of those kids who grew up in the church or anything like that, but I was introduced to God. I remember being introduced to God while living in Jamaica.

I went to a Catholic preparatory school and a Catholic high school. During those times, I participated in Catholic doctrine. I memorized the rosary, and I even once participated in dance for an event at the Catholic Church. While this was happening, I was also attending Saturday Bible study with a lady in Jamaica. However, the lady was not Catholic. I believe she was a Pentecostal. It was a group of us as kids who attended Bible study where she taught us about God. I was just happy to be around other kids and for the cookies that we would get after Bible study. While living in Jamaica, it was fair to say that I knew God.

When we moved to New York, we were residing with my cousin for a period of time. She always attended church, so we started going to church with her regularly. However, it was a Pentecostal Church, and this was a far fetch from the Catholic Church. It never seemed to bother me much. I just did what I was told and followed the rules of the religion. I got baptized at the age of 12 because I was constantly told that after 12, I would be responsible for my sins. I didn't want to have any sin, so I was striving to be perfect. That is why I wanted to be baptized.

I strived so hard that I even remember buying a bootleg copy of a Donnie McClurkin and a Yolanda Adams CD. I struggled so hard because I really wanted to listen to my Ashanti CD. So I started this crazy habit of listening to one type of music on certain days and gospel music on other days. It's quite funny now thinking about it, knowing how many sins I have. But this was just another situation of me knowing God.

I then moved to Florida and found a church to attend for a little while, but my family and I didn't have transportation so that didn't work out. Then I started to attend church with my oldest sister and that was pretty good. I would say it was a mega big church, but it was nondenominational. It was definitely different from what I was used to. While attending church there, I joined the church choir and even volunteered on a few occasions. Once again, I knew of God.

I went to college around 2006 and stayed in Florida. When I returned home, my mother and younger sister wanted me to join them at a new church they were attending. It was also nondenominational but had heavy Pentecostal influence. I attended church there regularly and was involved in the program and events when my school schedule allowed. I can honestly say that while attending this church, I began to realize that I was different and called for something great. However, even in that process, I only knew God.

While I was introduced to God at a fairly young age and had encountered several different religious beliefs and attended various churches, I only knew God. It wasn't until I got into business that I developed a relationship with God. Think about it this way, you meet someone and you go on dates with them, wine and dine with them, but you never commit to them. Well, that's how I was with God until I got into business.

Entrepreneuring.

I started my first company in 2014, which is my nonprofit, after deciding to pursue my goals. Here is the simplified story. I was told by someone that I was dating that I was not allowed to put my name on their company after I helped build it. The truth is, I was upset and decided to separate from that venture and pursue my goals. Having a non-profit organization was a part of that goal. Launching my nonprofit, Speak Loud Incorporated, was almost like the business warm-up before getting to the starting line of business; I learned a lot. Especially when it came to state laws, creating company policies, agreements and more. I learned how to be the leader of a team and how to be strategic to meet business goals. I also learned a very tough lesson of the importance of owning my business assets like my company domain name after having a web developer steal my domain name.

In 2015, I went through a time that I thought was the worst year of my life. I started to experience severe panic attacks triggered by work, numerous deaths in my family, a relationship breakup, and school stress as I was trying to complete my doctoral studies. I was having thoughts of suicide and considered crashing my car on countless occasions. After that, I went into complete depression and stopped driving for six months. I moved back in with my mom, sleeping on a twin-sized bed. She made me breakfast every morning and took it to my room just to make sure that I ate. And suddenly my biggest accomplishment became going to the pharmacy in my car by myself to pick up my prescription for Xanax and Zoloft and walking my dog.

My dad would tell me that he had been through something similar and the only way out of that dark place I was in was to consciously make an effort. So, somehow, I mustered up enough strength to drive without an anxiety attack and sign up to join the gym. I got a trainer and she allowed me to vent while working out and this was my starting line. Shortly after that, I came across a high school friend who was in business and helping individuals get clarity on their purpose. If there was anything else that I needed at that time, it was definitely clarity. So I signed up to work with her. Through our work, we birthed Priceless Planning, LLC.

I worked really hard to launch Priceless Planning, LLC. I spent countless hours, or in other words, I invested a lot of sweat equity into my business. I did my own branding and designed my logo and website. It was a hot mess, and it still took me what seemed like forever, as those are not my areas of expertise. However, as a proud graduate of YouTube University, I was committed to excellence, even while being a bootstrapping entrepreneur on a budget. I remember sitting in church on January 1, 2016 at 12 am, making my first social media post for my business from my phone. It was as if that was the time when God and I came into an agreement.

When I created the company, individuals told me it was not something I should take lightly. I never understood what they meant. I would even have individuals constantly tell me the company was not for me, it was for God, and I still didn't get it. It made absolutely no sense to me because frankly speaking, I am the planner, and everything is structured and will be done in my way. Through faith-based counseling, I learned how this ideology of mine had caused me unnecessary anxiety attacks. I wanted to be in control and not allow God. In other words, I was "tryna be grown."

When I started Priceless Planning LLC, it was only supposed to be an organizational consulting agency. That's all I wanted. So I was just going to have two companies: Priceless Planning LLC and Speak Loud Incorporated, my nonprofit. Jokes on me though as I had to quickly learn that God's Priceless Plan for my life is better than my Priceless Plan. I also had to learn that not every business coach is for me, and to allow God to handpick the ones He wants me to work with.

God will have you
make a fool of yourself
listening to everybody but Him.

Coaches.

Even if you are the smartest person in the world, in business, you are going to need help. Traditionally, when most people start a business, they automatically strive to work with a business coach. Nevertheless, as you're in business, you will need help. That help may come in the form of a business coach, financial coach, attorney marketing consultant, and more. But I have learned that those of us who are called for purpose are also assigned to follow the lead of specific people. We are also assigned certain people that will follow our lead.

However, who God wants for us to work with can quickly be overshadowed by the cool kids on social media. This is often where we learn some of our first mistakes in business. I realized that popularity is not always good and that the search for the hidden talents is worth it. I spent the first year in business working with multiple business coaches and mentors only to make $25 of revenue in my business, and I was not even able to pay myself from the business. I was investing a lot of my time and money, and seeing no returns, so I suffered a major financial loss.

In the second year of business, I was able to switch some strategies around. I chose to only work with people I felt divinely connected to and I finally broke even, but I was still not able to pay myself. While this is definitely progress because I didn't have a loss, something was wrong as I contemplated closing down many times. I felt so lost and disconnected from my business and only those closest to me knew it.

In the third year of doing business, I got frustrated with spending money on coaches and mentors and decided that I would trust my gut and build my business the way I wanted, based on what God placed in my heart. I decided that I was going to let go of all the validation I sought from others on how I should build my business. I decided that I was going to trust myself and quit behaving like a crazy person and placing the opinions of too many people in my business. I decided that I was going to allow God to be my business coach.

Making this decision came towards the end of my second year in business when I was feeling disconnected from my business. I met with a friend of mine to help me do some soul searching, and in that conversation, she told me something I did not expect to hear. She told me that I was not making time for God to hear from Him. She reminded me that while we do not love God for what He can do for us, there is a reciprocal relationship aspect that I was missing. There was an immediate sense of conviction that came upon me. I felt sick to my stomach and so guilty.

I wanted God to do so much for me financially so I could do for my family. But I was not praying and worshipping Him to the best of my abilities. This was such a one-sided relationship I wanted, but there was nothing I am giving in return. I knew Him, but I had no relationship, and God wanted my relationship, as it was no longer sufficient to just know Him. I was too busy hiring every coach, trying to get answers. But I was not busy asking God if these were the products and services I was supposed to be selling. I was not even asking God if what I was selling was in alignment with His will for me to serve others. I was not allowing Him to work through me. I was just doing what I wanted. I was basically being 'grown.'

I decided to change this behavior of mine, and the first thing I did was something that my friend recommended, which was to practice the art of gratitude. So, every morning for 30 days, I woke up and journaled about three things that I was thankful for in every aspect of life. I did not complain about what I did not have or what I wanted, but I was simply grateful. I started to realize that I had so much more to be grateful for and so many reasons to be worshipping God.

Well, it wasn't as if I did not know that God had been good to me, but I needed a reminder, and this was my reminder. Perhaps, this is why I felt disconnected from my business because I was not even grateful for my business. Perhaps, my business was not achieving the point of success that I wanted because I was being coached by everyone else and not God. I was reading every book except the Bible. I was in my way. God had to stop me in the middle of my tracks. It was like He paused my business and life so I could learn.

Pausing.

It was evident that the mission of my business needed to be changed. Here I was making the money, but I was not fulfilled. Almost every task that came with my business, began to carry a sense of burden and anxiety. Yet I pushed myself because I wanted to have that monetary gain and fame. So now, here am I, a fresh Ph.D. graduate, and ready to work full time in my already flourishing business. Yet again, I was still not obedient to changing the mission of my business.

At the end of 2018, I made my annual business plans because no matter what, I was going to be successful at being a full-time business woman. However, I noticed that something was wrong with my body as I didn't have my monthly woman gift for two months. I knew I wasn't pregnant, so I just ignored it and allowed for my body to run its course. However, in January of 2019, my monthly womanly gift returned with a vengeance. For 90 days, I was bleeding and it was intense, to say the least. But there was a day I would never forget.

I was feeling weak, had a cold and I automatically assumed that I had the flu because it was flu season. I took some medicine, drank lots of water. I was hydrated but I felt as if I was freezing and I began to experience chills and started shaking. I managed to pull myself up and went to take a hot shower to see if I could get warm. A hot shower turned into a bath, and as I sat down, I immediately threw up and felt like something was leaving my body. I couldn't breathe.

Confused on if I was overreacting, I called my family and asked to be taken to the hospital because that was not me. I got to the hospital and my blood pressure was low. Then, after a few more tests, I found out my hemoglobin was low, heart rate was high around 150, and I would be admitted for a blood transfusion. I sobbed and cried like a baby, as I believed I was going to die, more so, because I couldn't breathe and had to keep oxygen on.

I was in the hospital for four days and I couldn't do any type of business work. All I could do was call my assistant and let her know that I was out of the office. But as I was being discharged from the hospital, I felt somewhat better and was ready to go back to work. However, something was still not right, and I distinctly remember telling the nurse that was discharging me that I could not breathe. She told me not to worry. "Go home and get some rest. You will feel better." And that I did. However, the God was already one step ahead of the enemy and allowed me to have a previously scheduled doctor's appointment. When I arrived at the doctor's office, the nurses told me that I did not look like myself. In fact, my doctor also told me that she didn't like how I was looking and breathing. She had the nurse look check my vitals. And again I had a high heart rate, and was displaying signs of having difficulties breathing.

She immediately wrote a letter and instructed that I go to the emergency room and hand them that letter. I did exactly that and the nurses rushed me in a wheelchair to the back. After doing several tests, it was determined that I had double lung pneumonia. They gave me pneumonia medicine and I was allergic to the first one. The medicine broke me out in hives which aged uncontrollably. After five days of being admitted and being monitored to make sure that the CDC did not have to be called, I was finally discharged.

For the next six months, I was in and out of the hospital approximately 12 more times. I also needed blood transfusions and was having high blood pressure from pains. It was almost as if every time I tried to work on my business, I got sick. That means, for literally half of the year, I was in and out of the hospital and unable to be committed to my business. In the business world, that means I was broke. I had to drop clients, cancel contracts with my team, go ghost mode on my business' social media page, and cancel speaking engagements. My business was in shambles, as I was unable to be physically present. I mean, if God wanted me to be still, he could've just said it or perhaps I could've just listened the first time around.

But during one of my overnight hospital visits, I remember God speaking to me about my business. Specifically telling me that if nothing else is done for this year, endeavor to do at least what I have instructed you. I agreed, as I always joke with my family and friends and tell them that there are just some things I won't argue with God about. At that moment I knew that my business mission was not in alignment with the will of God.

My business mission for my nonprofit has never changed since its development in 2014; however, the business mission for my consulting agency has changed fifty times. With all those changes, I never once stopped and asked God if this was the mission that I should have for my business.

Duh, Sidjae! This is why you kept on
changing the business mission, as it was never in
alignment with God's plan, so you were never internally fulfilled.

For the next six months, I chose to not have a business mission and instead be obedient to what God was calling me to do at the moment. At the end of those six months, my business mission became clear. And when God gives you clarity, he will give you strategy.

God's strategy sounds wayyyyyy better than mine!

Strategy.

If there's nothing else that I have learned, at least I have learned that God's strategy is not common to the world. And yes, that is going to come with doing things that make you look like an absolute fool to others, but you do it anyway as you know you are being led by God. One of God's strategies that he gave me was for a book to be released. I followed his instructions and got help where I needed help, and the book made Best Seller one day after release.

It is important to note that when this book was released, I was in between one of the 12 hospital visits. To the world, I would've probably been told I needed to do 10 livestreams, book giveaways, and press tours. But instead, I released the book while on meds from the living room, weak and in sweats. My strategy during the release was to pray that the book reached those who needed it. Upon the book's release, there was a young lady who saw one of my sisters posting the book and purchased it. After reading the book, she told my sister that this book was exactly what she was looking for. She said that she needed to rebuild her relationship with God as she was giving up. At that moment, I realized that even if the book just sold one copy to her, I did my job. But how God chose to reward me was the title of a bestselling author.

Another strategy that God gave me was to have an international event. This was beyond crazy, as many people asked me why I didn't just have a local event before having an international event. The only answer I could give them is that God told me that, and I only have to obey. So I began event planning. I want you to keep in mind that this was my first ever live event. Every month during this event planning, God gave me a different scripture to stand firm on. Every scripture was given to me during a dream, and every day during each month I saw firmly how those scriptures applied to this event.

The scriptures were God's strategy to push me through completion of this event when I felt lost and my faith was weak. I even thought about canceling the event when anxiety tried to cripple me. However, after reflection, I realized it was never about my business. It was about spending time in His word as He already knew my needs to complete this mission. By the way, the event was beyond successful. The reviews were astounding, and the connections that made amongst participants were beyond anything I was capable of. It was all God.

Even the moments when I wanted to cancel the event came full circle, on the event day. Multiple people told me how far they traveled to attend the event. But there was one young man in particular who asked a question in the audience and shared his story. He mentioned that he traveled over two hours to get to the event. He stated that he was battling bipolar disorder, depression, and anxiety, and coming to the event showed him that he can get through anything with perseverance. Lastly, he said that speaking in public was not something he would do because of his anxiety, and being at the event he found his courage to do just that. After he shared his story the audience gave him a big applause. We could tell the immediate change in his self-esteem. Since the event, I have observed this young man make a 360 turn in a boost of confidence. So what if I quitted when it got tough?

These were all reminders that the event was never about me. It showed that God had a bigger purpose in mind and specific people who needed to be at the event. When it came to that event, all I imagined was just an event, but God had bigger plans of impact and a business opportunity. What I thought was my first event internationally, God spanned into an international business and a community of individuals that are dear to my heart. After all, what was I going to tell God? No, I won't do what He wants? God had a specific strategy for this event in mind that would benefit not just myself but also others.

That's the thing with God's strategy, it is different from the world's. They require us to spend time with Him and think of not just financial gains but also impact and effectiveness for His Kingdom. In the world of modern business, we can get so crippled as faith-based business owners to follow the strategies that the world creates. But what about the strategies that God is trying to give us? What about what He says? Perhaps we need to take the time to listen to the instructions that God is giving us. When did we get so caught up in creating our strategies? As faith-based business owners, we must put at the forefront of our minds that we are doing things based on what God says and not what the world says. We gain our business wisdom differently.

Wisdom.

But where can wisdom be found?

Where does understanding dwell?

No mortal comprehends its worth;

it cannot be found in the land of the living.

The deep says, "It is not in me";

the sea says, "It is not with me."

It cannot be bought with the finest gold,

nor can its price be weighed out in silver.

It cannot be bought with the gold of Ophir,

with precious onyx or lapis lazuli.

Neither gold nor crystal can compare with it,

nor can it be had for jewels of gold.

Coral and jasper are not worthy of mention;

the price of wisdom is beyond rubies.

The topaz of Cush cannot compare with it;

it cannot be bought with pure gold.

Where then does wisdom come from?

Where does understanding dwell?
It is hidden from the eyes of every living thing,
concealed even from the birds in the sky.
Destruction and Death say,

"Only a rumor of it has reached our ears."
God understands the way to it and
he alone knows where it dwells, for he views the
ends of the earth and sees everything under the heavens.
When he established the force of the wind
and measured out the waters.
When he made a decree for the rain
and a path for the thunderstorm,
then he looked at wisdom and appraised it;
he confirmed it and tested it.
And he said to the human race,
"The fear of the Lord—that is wisdom,
and to shun evil is understanding."

Job 28:1-28 NIV

Job 28 says the fear of the Lord is wisdom. This chapter in the Bible compares wisdom to different things on the earth. It strives to offer clarity on where exactly we can find wisdom. I didn't realize it, but I was gaining wisdom on how to go about business and life after I started fearing the Lord. It's a weird process to go through countless years running from your calling, trying one thing after the next until you are humbly forced to sit still in a corner, plan, and simply figure it out. I didn't realize it, but that's what was happening to me. Somewhere along the line, something shifted, and I began to have a deep concern about what God wanted. I started to have a concern about how many souls will be lost if I did not fulfill my calling. I started to think about what the wrath of God would look like if I did not do what he wanted.

After all, He never helped me with any of the things I wanted, as it was not in alignment with His will. Well, who knows? Probably that was just perfect timing. But it wasn't until I began to fear the Lord that I gained wisdom on how to go about my business. Whether it was daily devotions, worship, prayer, or even just reading a Bible plan, I sought Him. Once again in that process, I gained wisdom. My approach to life changed. I started to understand things as simple as why it was important to take care of His Temple. You know, I must say growing up in church, I constantly heard the phrase, "Your body is a temple." It was often referred to as abstaining from sex before marriage. However, it was when I got sick that I understood that it was more than that.

Taking care of His temple also meant eating properly, drinking more water, exercising, self-care, and counseling to protect my mental health. Isn't it ironic that most of us who grew up in the church never bothered to take care of His temple in that manner? However, it's important, and let me break it down in the simplest way. If you have health issues that you could have prevented, how can you fulfill your purpose? While all illnesses, physical and mental, are not self-inflicted wounds, let's be honest about a few things.

Could you have done something different to prevent/manage diabetes? Could you have done something different to manage your blood pressure? Could you have done something different to protect your mental health? Could you have exercised more to prevent heart disease? Could you have taken advantage of the free counseling sessions at your job? Could you have said no to that business collaboration so you wouldn't get overwhelmed and have anxiety attacks?

As I said before, not all health issues, physical or mental, are self-inflicted wounds, but if we can do our part and take care of His Temple, I'm certain that He will fulfill His promises of making sure that we are okay health-wise. Besides, not taking care of His Temple gives the enemy easier access to defeat us. I'm not a health expert, nor am I in the best physical shape, but what I know for certain is that we have to take care of His Temple by not just abstaining from sex, but also making sure that we are eating properly, drinking water, going to therapy, getting enough sleep, and practicing self-care.

This is my personal wisdom that I gained from seeking God. But if you can seek God and spend time with Him regularly, then you too can gain wisdom for the areas of your life in which God wants you to. He will even give you wisdom on how you should go about securing the bag, just like He did for me.

Securing tha bag without God will have you falling flat on your face.

Securing Tha Bag.

Now let's talk about why you're an entrepreneur. Is it just to secure the bag? Is it to save lives? Is it to impact others? Is it what God has ordained you to do? Is it because it is a new thing to do? Is it because you have no other option? I won't lie, when I started my business, it was just to secure the bag. Then it became something I was doing because I had no option. Now it's because I have finally realized that it is something that God has called me to do. But we'll talk about that later.

There was one specific occasion that I was about to give up on my business and I did my devotional. During that specific devotional, I read the story of the tower of Babel. It shifted my perspective and forced me to look inward for the reasons I was in business. The tower of Babel is a great story for entrepreneurs to read. Ideally, when you think entrepreneurs you think innovation. The tower of Babel being built was the greatest innovation of its time. Genesis 11:3-4 explains how the generation after Noah used innovation to create brick and mortar and built a tower to reach to the heavens.

They said to each other,

"Come, let's make bricks and bake them thoroughly."

They used brick instead of stone, and tar for mortar.

Then they said,

"Come, let us build ourselves a city,

with a tower that reaches to the

heavens so that we may make a name for ourselves;

otherwise we will be scattered over the face of the whole earth."

Genesis 11:3

So let's break this down. They had an idea. They wanted to build something. They built it in efforts to create a name for themselves. In other words, to gain fame. Never did they question if this idea was wrong, if it was led by God or their innate desires. They were able to build the tower, but to build it for fame was the wrong reason. It wasn't built on a Godly foundation. In Genesis 11:5-8, you will then see how God was displeased and chose to punish them.

When creating, it's important that we are building for God and not for innate desires. I believe that was why God made me pause. I was chasing rainbows, trying to get to the pot of gold and fulfilling my innate desires. I was not aligned with a Godly foundation, even though God placed purpose in my work. I was an entrepreneur building for the wrong reasons.

As a faith-based entrepreneur, there's absolutely no way everything could be done for free. However, there are points in your business where you will have to stop and realize that success does not always equal financial gains. These times will come when you have to be obedient to the voice of God and do what he wants. These are the moments when He may instruct you to give a scholarship away for your business program, turn your event into a free one, or keep doing the task He has assigned you to, even though you may only have one client or one sale.

While I understand the world tells us that if you have no clients or sales, you just have an expensive hobby, God says differently. He wants us to do good and gain wealth. With this in mind, it is important that we strive to do good in our business. Not just doing good when cameras are around for publicity, or to get social media likes, or even to go viral. But do good in our business because God has placed it in our hearts. For in the moments of doing good we realize that success does not always equal immediate financial gains, but there is a harvest that will be reaped from doing good.

Let us not become weary in doing good, for at the proper time we will reap a harvest if we do not give up.

Galatians 6:9 NIV

I will give you every place where you set your foot, as I promised Moses.

Joshua 1:3 NIV

Now you may be asking yourself the question of, how do we strike a balance between doing good and gaining wealth? It is simple. Create a business with a clear mission statement. Here are some examples of companies that are doing good. While grocery shopping, I picked up a bottle of Alfredo sauce, and to be honest, I had limited choices of Alfredo sauce because it was during the COVID-19 pandemic. When I got home, I noticed the bottle said donating 100% profits since 1982. I was truly impressed to see that a company found a way to be successful without financial gain.

We also know of Chick-fil-A for having great food and being closed on Sundays. We also know that they have great customer service and they obviously have financial gains. However, what is not widely known is that they also have tuition programs for their employees. These are success points that are not complementing a financial gain, but it is filled with obedience to God.

Then there is Warby Parker that donates a pair of glasses when you purchase a pair. These are all companies that are doing good. Whether they are faith-based or not, it is undeniable that they secured the bag and are using it to do good, while being profitable. So while we are in 'the bag', don't forget that God needs some of the coins from the bag to further His work and glorify His kingdom. When you do secure the bag, also remember that God manifested all you've accomplished, not you.

Manifest.

In the era of social media, anyone can create a page and quickly become an influencer from viral funny videos. However, with the 'crown' of influencer, it also means that individuals are teaching their personal beliefs to many. In other words, they lead and others follow. I've seen this commonly done when it comes to the term manifestation versus God being the one who manifests. We are being told that we hold power to manifestation when that is the furthest thing from the truth.

Deuteronomy 8:18-20 NIV

"But remember the Lord your God,

for it is he who gives you the ability to produce wealth,

and so confirms his covenant, which he swore to your ancestors,

as it is today. If you ever forget the Lord your God and follow

other gods and worship and bow down to them, I testify against

you today that you will surely be destroyed.

Like the nations the Lord

destroyed before you, so you will be destroyed for not obeying the

Lord your God."

The term manifestation was coined in the 19th century by a famous medium who believed that humans have the same power as Jesus. The term manifestation is also deeply rooted in the Laws of Attraction which is contradictory to the will of God. From its deep roots to its new-age use, it goes against what Paul discusses in Galatians 1 on how we are not supposed to practice any other gospel.

Galatians 1:6-7 NIV says,

"I am astonished that you are so quickly deserting the one who called you to live in the grace of Christ and are turning to a different gospel—which is really no gospel at all. Evidently, some people are throwing you into confusion and are trying to pervert the gospel of Christ."

If we've really had the power of manifestation to begin with, then what did we ever need God for? We must teach others that God manifests. God is the only one that holds the ultimate power of you being able to produce wealth and fulfill the dreams He has placed inside of you. As faith-based business owners, when we follow what the world says and try to manifest things on our own, we are going to fail. However, when we allow God to give us the ability to produce wealth, we will succeed.

In the era of social media, somehow, we are getting it confused by quickly deciding to follow those who are popular and are preaching manifestation without God. In other words, they are taking God out of the equation and telling you that you can do something on your own. And as we know, it is impossible to live in this world alone without the strength and health of God. It is also problematic when you are focusing on manifestation and creating a life for yourself that is outside the will of God. If you research the word, 'manifest station' and how it is being used in today's culture, you will notice that it focuses on you being the ultimate creator, the author, and the finisher of your life. But the Bible specifically tells us that God is the author, Creator, and finisher of our lives.

Hebrews 12:2 says,

"Looking unto Jesus the author and finisher of our faith;
who for the joy that was set before him endured the cross,
despising the shame, and is set down at the right
hand of the throne of God."

If we as faith-based entrepreneurs begin to believe that we can manifest (create our own), we are doing all the work without God. And if we are building anything without God, we will fail. The Bible even reminds us that we are not supposed to act in the flesh but in the spirit. It also warns us to be careful of those who are acting in the flesh and further redefines who we are as faith-based individuals.

Further, my brothers and sisters, rejoice in the Lord!
It is no trouble for me to write the same things to you again, and
it is a safeguard for you. Watch out for those dogs, those evildoers,
those mutilators of the flesh. For it is we who are the circumcision,
we who serve God by his Spirit, who boast in Christ Jesus,
and who put no confidence in the flesh —

Philippians 3:1

If you are serving God, acknowledging His goodness, and not saying that you did it all on your own, God will help you, even if you are unqualified.

Answer God's call.
Even if you're
unqualified.

Unqualified.

My grandma told me that my grandpa's mom was a house slave. That means that two generations of relatives before me were slaves. It takes an enormous amount of work to break the generational cycles and curses that comes with slavery. A lot of the opportunities I have, my parents did not. So almost everything I have done in my life is uncharted waters and is led by no other than God.

My parents never went to college, and they did what they had to do to take care of me and my sibling. When I was born, they were immigrants to the U.S., determined to make sure my sibling and I did the right thing so we didn't have to struggle in our adult life like them. Based on my family upbringing, I am unqualified. I was unqualified to go to college, earn a doctoral degree, and start a business, but I did it. I was also unqualified to be a best-selling author and take over 25 authors to best-seller status. But I seem to have done it too.

There is a small percentage of individuals who make it out of broken family dynamics because they are unqualified. There is no family mentorship to give the prerequisites for how to get things done. There is no family business to pass down, no blueprint, and definitely no family business loan. The lack of resources leaves many stuck in an unqualified space for opportunity and growth.

But I am obedient to the things God tells me to do. My obedience has allowed God to take me, the unqualified, to get work done for His kingdom. A lot of things that I do today and have on my goal list to get done, I am unqualified for. But I seem to have repeatedly proven to myself that if God gives me a vision, He will find the provisions to ensure that I am qualified to meet the goals He has placed within me.

I look at situations where I became the best-selling author, having about 1000 followers on social media. To the world I was unqualified, but God provided me with people who would ensure that I met the goal He gave me. Or even the time I landed a deal with a multimillion-dollar company. They specifically told me that they had no clue how I made it to their radar. I laughed in my heart and said, "God," as it is not typical that after only a few years of consulting I should be landing companies such as these for my clients.

You have to realize that God will give you assignments even when you are unqualified. However, the only way to complete the assignment is through His strategy. His strategy qualifies you. Most importantly, His strategy will allow others to see the work of God in your life. Your obedience even when you are unqualified means that you could be winning souls for the kingdom. God has always proven Himself to use the unqualified for some of His biggest projects.

David committed adultery.

Noah was an alcoholic.

Rahab was a prostitute.

Peter denied Jesus.

...and the list goes on.

What I know for sure is that God chose to use them all for great things, despite their reckless behaviors, and poor life choices, which made them unqualified. If you are feeling unqualified for your path to entrepreneurship, remember that God calls the unqualified to qualify them. Many entrepreneurs are unqualified for the calling. However, many are obedient to what God wants them to do and are committed to making sure that they do it His way.

Calling.

For the longest time, I had no clue that my business could be my ministry. From growing up in the shadows of religion, I thought that if I was not a preacher in a church that my work would never be considered good enough for God. I thought it meant that I was on the outside of what God wanted from me. Somewhere along the line, I was told that my business was my calling and God wanted me to do it. Then I started to see and understand how my calling was contributing to God's kingdom. Also, in the middle of doing what God wanted me to do, I started seeing my business helping people rebuild their relationship with God. At first, I was completely shocked, but then during a sermon at my church, my pastor spoke on the body of Christ and its functions from

Roman 12:3-8

It states,

"For by the grace given to me I say to every one of you:
Do not think of yourself more highly than you ought,

but rather think of yourself with sober judgment,

in accordance with the faith God has distributed to each of you.

For just as each of us has one body with many members,

and these members do not all have the same function,

so in Christ we, though many, form one body,

and each member belongs to all the others.

We have different gifts, according to the

grace given to each of us.

If your gift is prophesying, then prophesy

in accordance with your faith; if it is serving, then serve;

if it is teaching, then teach; if it is to encourage, then give

encouragement; if it is giving, then give generously;

if it is to lead, do it diligently; if it is to show mercy, do it cheerfully.

After reading this, I finally understood how my business is a ministry that would play a vital role in the body of Christ. I also understood how other individuals and their callings were to play a vital role in the body of Christ. I then started researching Christian leaders, business owners, and learning more about what they did in their businesses to contribute to the body of Christ.

I got it!

The simple fact that my business was creating opportunities to hire individuals, that means I was putting food on their tables for their families. I was being used as a vessel of God to answer prayers. The fact that my business was helping individuals share their stories and birth their businesses or ministries meant that I was having a generational impact. I was being used as a vessel of God to create change. The fact that my business was helping minority and at-risk youth meant that I was helping to break generational curses. I was being used as a vessel of God to intercede on behalf of others.

After years of trying to understand why I was this multi-passionate person, I finally understood that God wanted to use me as a vessel. I finally understood why the devil was so mad and I encountered numerous spiritual attacks. So I ask you, what is your calling? How is your calling playing a vital role in the body of Christ? It's important that you do not let others tell you that your dream is too far-fetched.

You may be the next shoe designer helping pastors achieve comfort while they preach. You may be the next hospital owner creating a safe zone for individuals to receive fair treatment in the healthcare system. You may even be the next school principal advocating for the rights of children in your community. You may be the next scientist finding a cure for cancer. Or you may even be a community gardener providing low-income families with fresh fruits and vegetables at no cost. All of these examples and more contribute to the body of Christ, depending on the lens you choose to see it through.

What's important to note is that your calling may not be in the entrepreneurial field. Well, I know this is very hard to believe, as becoming an entrepreneur is a new trend. However, all of us are not called to do the same. But it's important that you answer your calling and contribute to playing your vital role in the body of Christ. If you have gifts that should be used for entrepreneurship purposes, use them. I believe that's one way for us to worship God and show our appreciation for His blessings.

Using my gifts for
His kingdom.

Gifts.

A man's gift maketh room for him,
and bringeth him before great men.

Proverbs 18:16 KJV

Your gifts are what will take you into your purpose and create financial opportunities for you. It was hard for me to understand this. Especially being that I have more than one gift. But being a multi-passionate entrepreneur, I struggled. I struggled with what I should launch first and what I should be doing simultaneously. I didn't know when to stop or when to go. I even struggled with whether to listen to others or stay in my lane. I tried to make all of my gifts fit in one lane.

I searched high and low for advice, often ignoring the will of God and what he told me to do. Of course, every time I was disobedient, I would fall flat on my face. Somehow, I forgot that God made a promise that my gift will make room for me and bring me before great men. There are many individuals in the Bible whose gift has made room for them. Let's look at the story of the widow and the prophet Elisha.

2 Kings 4:1-7 NIV speaks about the widow who cried out to the prophet Elisha for help. The widow's husband died owing some debts, and the debt collectors were coming for collaterals since the debt was not repaid. The collateral was her two sons being used as slaves. The prophet Elisha asked the widow what she had in her house, and the widow replied that she had a small jar of olive oil.

Let's consider the small jar of olive oil to be her gift. I will further explain how the widow's gift was used for her purpose and to create financial opportunities.

Business Funding-The prophet Elisha then instructed the widow to ask her neighbors for empty jars.

The Hustle-The prophet Elisha then told the widow to go inside her house and pour oil into each of the jars. So the widow did just that. She hustled hard to fill the jars.

The Team-But in verse 5, it said, "They brought the jars to her and she kept pouring." (Emphasis on 'they'). This means her sons were her team members.

God's Provision for Your Gifts·Verse 6 says, "When all the jars were full, she said to her son, "Bring me another one." But he replied, "There is not a jar left." Then the oil stopped flowing." It doesn't take a mathematical genius to know that the widow's small jar of olive oil could not have filled all of those jars. But God provided enough oil to fill the jars so she could start her business.

Launch Day·The prophet Elisha then told the widow to go and sell the oil to pay her debts.

The Profit·Verse 7 said, "You and your sons can live on what is left." Not only did the widow and her son sell and pay their debts, but they also got a profit too. Talk about financial opportunities!

Imagine if the widow never took the advice of the one God sent to help her.

Imagine if the widow filled all the jars by herself without a team.

Imagine if the widow had faith but no work and therefore did not want to hustle.

Imagine if the widow was not strategic in
getting business funding and tools.

Imagine how many families would have been without oil if the
widow only created the product but did not want to sell.

Imagine the lives her son would have had if they went into slavery
because of her not listening to the one that God sent to help her.
Imagine if the widow operated outside of this specific order.

God wants us to identify our gifts, realize how that fits into our purpose, and He will ensure that we have financial opportunities to thrive. But in using our gifts and understanding how it fits into our purpose, we still have to be open to a few things like listening to those that God sends our way to help us, stop trying to do it all on our own, have faith, and take action.

Your gifts are bigger than you. Your gifts have a purpose and they will align for your greater good. Your gifts are what will take you into your purpose and create financial opportunities for you. Your purpose is what God needs you to live out so you can save souls for His kingdom. Some people may just have one gift and others may have multiple gifts. Just know they will make room for you.

Multipassionate.

If I had my choice, I would be a hairstylist. That's because in my head I think it is a financially rewarding business. However, I cannot fix anyone's hair except my own. If I had my choice, I would also have a career in the medical field. Perhaps a surgeon or a renowned doctor. However, I am not good at science. In fact, I've always struggled in that area. Even in high school, I struggled with environmental science. However, you know what, I am good at planning. I have been planning since I was in high school. I'm also very good at being organized and structured, helping others get organized, and creating structures for others. I'm also very good at helping others understand their career choices for life, creating budgets, conducting research, analyzing qualitative data and writing stories. I'm also really good at operating in more than one avenue at a time.

So when I started my business and I consistently heard that I should stay in one lane, I was brokenhearted. But I tried it because you know, the 'experts' said so. I followed what the experts said and not what God said. I forgot that I was uniquely made. My choice to follow what the experts said also made me take my business away from the presence of God. The Bible speaks about this in

Psalms 139:7-15 NIV

Where can I go from your Spirit?
Where can I flee from your presence?
If I go up to the heavens, you are there;
if I make my bed in the depths, you are there.
If I rise on the wings of the dawn,
if I settle on the far side of the
sea, even there your hand will guide me,
your right hand will hold me fast.
If I say, "Surely the darkness will hide me
and the light become night around me,"
even the darkness will not be dark to you;
the night will shine like the day,
for darkness is as light to you.
For you created my inmost being;
you knit me together in my
mother's womb.

I praise you because I am fearfully and
wonderfully made; your works are wonderful,
I know that full well. My frame was not hidden from you when I
was made in the secret place, when I was woven together
in the depths of the earth.

When I look back in my life, I see that God was always preparing me to be a multi-passionate person. It's just how He made me, even though since I was young, I thought there was something wrong with me. But this also explains why I was never able to leave the desire to tackle more than one thing at once. The desire to be multi-passionate has always been within me as something that God was preparing me for from a young age. When I was young, I wanted to be a tennis champion like the young Serena Williams I was seeing on TV. In that very same year, I also wanted to be a cheerleader and run for class president. I tried my hand at all three. By the way my family will never let go of the fact I had them go all over to find a tennis racket, or wrap pencils with my name on them as campaign collateral, and how can I forget coming home late from cheerleading practice.

Then there was also the time in high school where I was doing chorus, involved in student government, and apart of the senior class board. When I got to college, this trend never seemed to leave me, so I was also in multiple organizations on different spectrums. You know what, to take it back even further, when I was in the 6th grade in Jamaica, I was playing netball. I was also the Head girl and a Prefect. Through all of those situations and more, I was constantly told I needed to choose one thing. So when I became a "grown-up," I thought I needed to choose yet again. This belief led me to have moments where I was completely stuck and honestly unfulfilled.

So if you're like me...a multi-passionate human, I just want you to know it's ok to not 'stay in one lane'. And yes, you can have a business or businesses that encompasses all of your passions. My biggest tip is to make sure it's well planned and organized. In fact, each of my business ventures falls within strategic legal and financial structures. That is also coupled with its organizational structure, business model, branding, and more. I was serious when I told you I really love planning and organizing. Additionally, I want to make sure that I'm presenting to the world God's gifts that He has placed on the inside of me the best way possible.

Lastly, the takeaway here for the multi-passionate people is to make sure that you are not choosing to pursue careers or business ventures outside of the presence of God. You know...chasing rainbows and pursuing the bag outside the will of God. Also, make sure to follow what God says and not what 'experts' say. And in all that you do, strive for excellence.

Excellence...
it's a Kingdom thing!

Excellence.

Give your purpose your all. That's what it means to operate in excellence. Just like how surgeons commit to providing excellent surgeries to patients, or an attorney commits to helping clients win a case, you should also be committed to excellence within your business, especially if you are a Believer. Whether you are serving one client or 10,000, the same level of excellence should be delivered. Anything less than excellence is not a true reflection of God. Do you know how embarrassing it is to the body of Christ when one person does something poorly in the business God has gifted them? The first thing we always hear is:

"Oh, she is a Christian, and this is how she does business."

Do you know that to have someone speak this way about the way you operate your business can change the heart of a non-believer from giving their life to Christ? It can make them walk away from their faith in which they were already struggling. Our goal as faith-based entrepreneurs is not just to operate a business to generate wealth, it is also to be Christ-like in all that we do.

When Jesus was on Earth, He ensured everything He did was a reflection of God. He operated in excellence and that can be seen throughout the Bible. Whether He was fighting for justice and saving the Israelites or feeding a crowd with five fishes and two loaves of bread, He operated in excellence.

When He was saving the Israelites, He could have decided to bring them to the Red Sea and not part it. But imagine how that could make the Israelites lose their faith in God because He did not operate in excellence. When He was feeding a crowd with five fishes and two loaves of bread, He could have designed some sort of lottery system, limiting the number of people that would be fed, but He decided to operate in excellence and feed everyone that was there.

Whether your business is to create a logo, make a meal, maintain financial records, or even file for trademarks and patents, make sure that you are operating in excellence. To attain excellence, I worked hard in ensuring that product deliveries are made on time, not misusing clients' info, or submitting paperwork on time based on when the client paid for it.

Let's take for example; if you are an accountant and you are supposed to ensure that your clients' bookkeeping is up-to-date and taxes are being paid on time, and for the past three months, you have been traveling the world and not staying up-to-date with your clients' financial books, and the taxes you told the client to pay are inaccurate because you rushed through the work. Now, your client has to pay the government a large lump sum of money to get everything sorted out. This has also forced your clients into laying off two of his employees to make room within the budgets to pay the government fees. Well, what you didn't know is that two employees were laid off, and now they don't have meals on their tables for their children and have lost hope in God.

While some people consider these to be customer service issues, and that they are, these simple tasks are held to a different standard when you are a faith-based entrepreneur as it can make or break someone. So do you want to be the person operating in excellence and as a reflection of God?

Law.

Faith as we know is not seen, it is the act of belief. You tell God that you want to become a surgeon. You have faith and you are believing that God will help you become a surgeon. Two years pass by and you're having faith but you're not a surgeon yet. You're upset with God because you had faith and He hasn't rewarded you yet. But shouldn't you be upset with yourself? In those two years, what have you done to exercise your faith?

There's a common misconception that faith is disobedient to the law of the land. Or even better said that faith disregards the law of the land. If we look at the steps (based on the law of the land) that are required to become a surgeon, it may include getting a bachelor's degree, going to medical school, going through a residency program, and then becoming a surgeon.

Now through this process from the law of the land, we will need to have faith. Have faith that God will carry us through the process and give us the wisdom to pass any exams, as well as favor for getting a job. However, somewhere in life, we have become a set of people who have forgotten that God is still obedient to the law of the land, as He is a God of order. Being a God of order also means that He expects us to have faith and take the necessary steps to fulfill our purpose (including following the law of the land). So if you know that your purpose involves becoming a business owner, why haven't you been showing God that you are exercising your faith?

Exercising your faith may look like getting your business license, hiring expert help, and signing up for online courses to further expand your knowledge. But it's almost as if we expect God to leave His throne to come down to earth, hold our hands and take us to go get the business license, hire the expert help, and sign up for the online courses. Some people are just so stuck on having faith that they become stagnant. You've had faith for five years now, yet you have done nothing else. You have to realize that following the law of the land is a part of having faith.

Then we also have to look at another part of the law of the land when it comes to our business. Let's call this business maintenance. There are many things that we will have to do as business owners to maintain what God has given us. It may be renewing a business license, filing annual reports, using wisdom to legally protect ourselves, and paying our taxes. In fact, Romans 13: 1-7 explains how we are supposed to be responsible citizens and follow the governing authorities over the land. Let's take for example Roman 13 verse 7, which reminds us that we are supposed to pay our debts and taxes.

Give to everyone what you owe them: If you owe taxes, pay taxes; if revenue, then revenue; if respect, then respect; if honor, then honor.

Romans 13:7 NIV

But prior to this verse, we are warned about what will happen if we don't follow the law of the land.

Consequently, whoever rebels against the authority is rebelling against what God has instituted, and those who do so will bring judgment on themselves.

Romans 13:2 NIV

As faith-based entrepreneurs, we should be setting an example for others on how to follow the law of the land when it comes to business. We should not be withholding taxes, committing fraud, or scamming individuals out of their hard-earned money. Those who do this and disobey the law of the land will embarrass the body of Christ when judgment is brought upon them.

In today's world, we know that everything makes it to social media. Imagine being a viral topic on social media for tax evasion or scamming individuals out of money. Because you chose to disobey the law of the land and not do the right thing, you caused judgment upon yourself.

Do you know what that does to the lost children of God? Do you know how that impacts the reputation of other faith-based entrepreneurs? You have to realize that not everything in your business is about you. Remember that your business is a gift from God and that He is trusting you with it to do the right thing, even when it's easier to do wrong. This is why it is extremely important that we follow the law of the land as an act of faith, and also to not cause judgment upon ourselves.

Faithing Forward

Fear.

I was waiting for my biggest deal to come through and you know what came over me, FEAR. I was confident that I knew the work very clearly. Of course, I have a Ph.D. in the subject matter, and I spent years on years in multiple jobs that also gave me practical information and experience. So, what was wrong with me? I was scared out of my mind to close a six-figure deal. At first, I struggled with being able to close the deal, so I went through a 3-day intensive process to make sure that I had enough knowledge on how to get the deal. Then it came to the morning of meeting for the deal, I was scared again and filled with silly thoughts of *'what if they don't like me?'*

The morning of the deal, I was unintentionally reminded of a scripture from 2 Corinthians by an app on my phone. I was also reminded that I cannot walk in both faith and fear at the same time. With no time to debate with myself, I clearly had to choose faith, and as I like to say, #faithforward. After all, I had been stressing God out praying morning, noon, and night for something good to happen. I prayed for Him to make a way in my business so that I can create an operating expense budget at least for the next two years which would be sufficient. I wanted to be able to pay myself consistently and also wanted two employees, full-time with benefits.

The truth is, I had gotten to a point where I had to admit to God that I was struggling to manage the different purposes that he gave me, and if he wanted me to fulfill the purposes, then I would need help. And of course, getting the help, you need money. So I told God that this business had to work or it's back to a 9-5. I truly believe that God must have laughed at me and wondered what was wrong His child. I also knew that deep down He understood my level of frustration.

I went into the deal meeting and did an amazing presentation on a Tuesday. They told me they would get back to me by Monday, as they had to speak to their executive team. Well, they got back to me on Friday with a Yes. This was a pivotal place for me in business, as I completely changed the trajectory for how I was developing my business. It reassured me that I was headed in the right way all along and God had me covered. It was important because I received this deal during a season when the world was going through so much to say the least. I'm talking about when the world was going through a pandemic that affected the financial well-being of many; but I was still able to close a deal.

But something happened to me. When I got the deal, a sense of fear came upon me. I was worried if I would be overwhelmed with the work that I was being tasked. I began to worry and question myself about all the things that could go wrong. What if I start to have anxiety attacks again? What if I spend too much money and not save enough for my taxes? What if I hire too quickly, and then run out of money in my operating budget? What if they're not pleased with my service?

And the list goes on and on for the worries that came my way. But I had to realize that I was operating in a spirit of fear and it was causing me to panic. It was almost like, here I was, finally out of my drought season, having everything that I prayed for; what was I afraid of? Then I unintentionally came across this scripture:

"...but of power, and of love, and of a sound mind."

2 Timothy 1:7 NIV

And I was reminded that God gives me power, stability, and strength. It was clear that if God had called me to this type of work and alignment with my purpose, he must have known that I had the strength to see it through. When it comes to facing your fears in business, I have realized that it causes us to waste God's time. We are asking God for opportunities, yet we are not ready. Many of us are pouring out our tears to God begging for God to bless us. Yet we have fears, either doubting what God is capable of doing or fearful of our inability to manage the blessing. We have to remember that if God has called us to use our gifts, then there's nothing to be afraid of.

Have not I commanded thee? Be strong and of good courage;
be not afraid, neither be thou dismayed: for the Lord thy God is
with thee whithersoever thou goest.

Joshua 1:9 NIV

If God has called you to the task of being in business, then it shows that He trusts your ability to manage the tasks and He is confident in what He will do. When God called Joshua as leader over the Israelites, He made him a promise to give him everywhere that he set his foot, just as He did to Moses. He also instructed him to be strong, courageous, and a law-abiding citizen. Joshua released his fear, did as God told him, and received God's protection.

God gave Joshua the strategy of marching around Jericho and protected him from the enemy while he marched. God even gave Joshua the strategy of how to take ownership of royal cities, and while Joshua executed the strategy, God protected him. However, we have to realize that Joshua was able to move forward after he released his fear.

Protection.

One night I had a dream that reminded me of God's protection over my life and purpose. In the dream, I was in a war zone and people were fighting; there was smoke and chaos. I was running and a man reached out to me and said, "Go this way, I will hide you here." I went into a corner and hid. The people fighting ran past where I was hiding. I was left unharmed and the man who hid me told me, "You can go now, it's safe."

When I woke up from the dream, I felt different knowing that God got me. He was and still is covering me for my purpose, which for me is within my business. Just like how He protected the Israelites when they walked through the middle of the sea in efforts to be freed from the Egyptians.

But the Israelites walked right through the middle of the sea on dry ground, the waters forming a wall to the right and the left. God delivered Israel that day from the oppression of the

Egyptians. And Israel looked at the Egyptian dead,

washed up on the shore of the sea.

Exodus 14:29-31 MSG

God is a protector over every area of our lives, including our businesses. He will close doors for business deals when it is not in our best interest. He is doing this because He is protecting us. While we may only see a missed revenue opportunity, God is one step ahead releasing his protection. Hearing my first no for a collaboration years ago made me boohoo as this 'woman' belittled me because I didn't fit in with the hype crowd. But that rejection was God's protection. So, the reality is, you have to brace yourself for the no and get ready to drop jaws when you get the yes from the most unexpected people; the yes from the people who you have never met or only met once, or even just online friends.

In the end, it's all a part of God's protection plan. But more importantly, sometimes God is protecting us from ourselves. He knows that should He give some of us certain opportunities when we want it, we would not know how to act. We see this all too common in the online digital space of business. Someone who was all about God before 'they made it', and then dropped God 'like it's hot' when they made it. God blessed them and they forgot Him.

I have met some great friends in business who have received opportunities to work with celebrity clientele. They are some of the most humble souls. I tell them all the time that if I was them, I would get a t-shirt made and wear it every day. I would be so extra on my bragging rights. Then I normally say, that's why God ain't ready for me yet with certain things because I need work.   But the reality is, should I be bragging about God's goodness in my life and the opportunities He has created for me through my obedience? Versus me bragging about who I have worked with. God will protect you from yourself so you don't embarrass His kingdom. Or He will strip you of your accomplishments to protect you from yourself so you can learn to be humble.

See, that's the thing about chasing rainbows, it will have you going after the wrong things. Chasing the rainbow to not only secure the bag, but also the fame and the bragging rights.

And I know you probably are saying to yourself, oh, that's not me. But God knows us more than we even know ourselves. This is why He protects us from the enemy and ourselves. It took me a while to realize how God was not only protecting me from the enemy but also bad business deals, partnerships, and even myself. When I finally understood it, I no longer got upset when things didn't work out the way I planned. I also noticed a shift that took place in my business, and God started to open new doors for me. He has sent me some high-end clients to work with. It's actually a weird feeling when God starts giving you the unexpected because He realizes that you're growing in Him with your business. It's almost as if sunshine is coming out over your business.

After the storm
the rainbow comes.

Sunshine.

So you've weathered through the business storm. You saw the rainbow and now you are running your way to "the promised pot of gold." I mean, after all, the sunshine is about to come out. Waiting for the sun to come out in your business is a process. I wish I could tell you that it was all roses and lilies and everything was easy. I wish I could tell you that the process is one that will be over in just a day or two. For some of us, we may reach our financial goals within a year, for others, it may take five years. That is why it is important that we don't chase rainbows but instead chase our purpose. As cliché as this may sound, each of us has our purpose and calling in our path.

But perhaps there are specific steps and instructions that we are supposed to receive on our respective paths. This is why it is important to believe that everything aligns in your life for your greater being, Romans 8:38. The hardest part about business is probably the wait time. You are waiting for your fruits to harvest, waiting to reap what you have been sowing, waiting to see the blessings from all of your hard work and obedience. It's literally a process of waiting for the sun to come out after going through everything.

In this process, it is going to be really important that you have faith. Also, it is really important that you believe and realize that your purpose is bigger than the waiting process. Once again, that is why it's important to chase your purpose and not rainbows. Changing the way we think is the only way in which we can endure the process. In changing the way we think, we have to constantly renew our minds. That is why it's important to have our daily devotion with God our time of Bible study, our intimate time of hearing his voice, and of course our time of prayer.

Do not conform to the pattern of this world, but be transformed by the renewing of your mind. Then you will be able to test and approve what God's will is — his good, pleasing, and perfect will.

Romans 12:2 NIV

It helps us in staying steadfast in the promises of God.

Romans 4:20-22 NIV says,

Yet he did not waver through unbelief regarding the promise of God, but was strengthened in his faith and gave glory to God, being fully persuaded that God had the power to do what he had promised. This is why "it was credited to him as righteousness."

The words, "It was credited to him", were written not for Him alone, but also for us, to whom God will credit righteousness—for us who believe in Him who raised Jesus our Lord from the dead. Don't stay stuck in feeling like there is no possible way that God is in your business. Rather believe that He has a purpose for you, and you are waiting on the promises at the end of the rainbow. He reminds you in **Romans 5:1-4 NIV** that you should have peace, hope, and perseverance.

Therefore, since we have been justified through faith,
we have peace with God through our Lord Jesus Christ,
through whom we have gained access by faith into
this grace in which we now stand.
And we boast in the hope of the glory of God.
Not only so, but we also glory in our sufferings,
because we know that suffering produces perseverance;
perseverance, character; and character, hope.

So while waiting for the sun to come out, God gives you grace while you're standing and provides you with perseverance to get through your sufferings, which will lead to you having a stronger character and faith. While culture teaches us that we are to become overnight millionaires. It is not realistic and this teaching is why so many give up when it gets tough. But **Romans 12:12 KJV** says we are to be,

Rejoicing in hope;

patient in tribulation;

continuing instant in prayer;

That's a pretty heavy word to receive but it definitely reassures us that it is okay to wait and know that everything is working out for our greater good. But our blessings will come at the cost of our obedience in our business.

Obedience.

There's something to be said about obedience and God. As faith-based entrepreneurs, business owners, and leaders, we have to realize that God instructs us when we are to move and do certain things. He will give us the exact moment in which we should launch. He will give us the words of our launch. He will give us the next product to develop. He will make sure that we're at the right place and time to meet the right person, and also make sure that our clients find us. But it all starts at one thing, and that is OBEDIENCE.

What if the Israelites were not obedient to God when he promised them that He would lead them to freedom? What if they considered Him to be crazy when He told them to put the blood on their doorpost, or when He told them to bake bread in preparation to leave? If they were never obedient, they would have never seen God's promises. Isn't that something to think about? Many times as a faith-based entrepreneur, God is telling us to use uncommon strategies, methods, techniques, and we don't listen and honestly end up falling flat on our faces.

Around 2019, my business made a shift as I was becoming obedient to God and the strategies that he gave me. Yes, some of them seemed outright crazy and made no sense to me, but I decided to trust. After all, I was left with no choice when I realized I was failing. But the act of being obedient is also going to require that we have faith. We have to trust and believe that even though we don't see the big picture, God is leading us the right way. I often hear folks say that faith and fear cannot reside together. But you know what can? Faith and obedience.

In the season of Passover, whether you celebrate it or not, you cannot deny its significance and the many acts of faith that the Israelites did to have faith that God would free them. From placing blood on the doorpost to baking bread in preparation for God's promises of freedom to be received, they were acting in faith. In fact, even when they left the bread behind, it was another act of faith as they trusted that if God was freeing them, He would provide for them. They were #faithingforward! I'm sure God must have seen them as filled with faith. They believed His promises no matter how many plagues they saw happening. They continuously prepared in faith for their freedom. Most of all, they were being obedient to what God told them to do in preparation for Him to lead them to freedom.

Just like you, I saw the social media posts of many claiming their way to the top. Many bragging, and making it look so easy. No one ever really talks about the grit of entrepreneurship. How you lose friends; how sometimes you are doing the work and not seeing the coins; how it's scary knowing that you have to keep revenue coming in to maintain an operational budget to pay yourself and your team, oh! And the tax bill. No one talks about the tax bill. No sah *(Jamaican dialect for no way... 'cause I really had no other way to express it)*.

Listen, if I had it my way, I would have quit many times. But... I am obedient. Do you ever wonder what would have happened if the people in the Bible weren't obedient?

God asked Noah to build the ark. Then asked me to build my business.

Noah.

The story of Noah is probably one of the most popular stories in the Bible. Noah was obedient, even when he didn't understand what God was telling him to do. The moments when it made no sense, when his actions were not popular, when people mocked him; he was getting crazy, but he was still obedient to God. Building the Ark was Noah's purpose. God gave him the blueprint on how to build the ark. He gave him the measurements for the ark, what type of material to use, where to put the doors, and what type of roof to build. He even told him what animals to bring and who to bring on the ark. He told him when to go on the ark. God gave Noah the details to his purpose, and it was up to him to act in obedience. Noah was obedient. His obedience was mentioned twice in his story.

Noah did everything just as God commanded him.

Genesis 6:22 NIV

And Noah did all that the Lord commanded him.

Genesis 7:5 NIV

Noah's obedience gave him protection and allowed God to make a promise to mankind. Only after gaining wisdom can you understand how obedience can offer protection. Noah's obedience protected him and his family while God was wiping every living thing off the face of the Earth. Ask yourself this question. What would have happened if Noah was not obedient and did not build the ark? How would that have affected mankind and civilization? **Genesis 7:23 NIV** explains how Noah was protected after God sent the floods.

Every living thing on the face of the earth was wiped out; people and animals and the creatures that move along the ground and the birds were wiped from the earth. Only Noah was left, and those with him in the ark.

Also because of Noah's obedience, God made a promise to mankind.

I establish my covenant with you: "Never again will all life be destroyed by the waters of a flood; never again will there be a flood to destroy the earth."

Genesis 9:11 NIV

God reminds us of this promise with a rainbow.

"I have set my rainbow in the clouds,
and it will be the sign of the covenant
between me and the earth.
Whenever I bring clouds over the earth and the rainbow
appears in the clouds, I will remember my covenant between me
and you and all living creatures of every kind. Never again will
the waters become a flood to destroy all life.
Whenever the rainbow appears in the clouds,
I will see it and remember the everlasting covenant between God
and all living creatures of every kind on the earth."

Genesis 9:13

But what if Noah disobeyed God? What if he never built the ark? Would God have still protected him from the floods? Would God have made the same promise to mankind? I don't know about you. But a lot of scenarios played out in my head. So I have to ask you these questions.

Are you being obedient to what God is telling you about your purpose? Are you being obedient and developing your business the way God tells you to? Or are you doing it the way of the world? If you don't do what God is telling you to do, who will be impacted? How can you be obedient like Noah over your purpose and business? It's time for us to admit to ourselves that trying to secure the bag outside the will of God will bring forth specific revelations. Revelations that will call us and our business back home into the will of God for the glory of His kingdom.

Revelations.

Business is not what you see online. You only see one-third of a business online. There is an enormous amount of work that goes into business. You can also lose yourself, your mental health, your friends, and your family while trying to build a business. You are even more subjected to facing these situations if you are solely focused on securing the bag and not the will of God.

It's important that we follow the will of God for our lives. To me, this is a safe spot. As it allows for me to do what I have to do so God can do what he needs to do. I find comfort in knowing that I am upholding my end of the deal, and my faith in God reassures me that he will uphold his end of the deal. Taking this approach allowed me to rid my life of unnecessary stressors. It allowed me to relinquish control of my business back into the hands of God.

Just like any other profession, if you are called by God to do business, you must be obedient and complete his work and efforts to glorify the kingdom. I don't believe that entrepreneurship is for everyone. This is why some quit before the work even starts. I do strongly believe that there are individuals who are called to use their gifts in entrepreneurship. Having this calling allows for these chosen individuals to be protected against the attacks of the enemy and withstand the pressures that come with the territory.

Whether you have a calling to entrepreneurship, being a doctor, a singer, or any other profession, it's important to note that with your obedience, God will give you what He promised.

I will give you every place where you set your foot,
as I promised Moses.

Joshua 1:3 NIV

However, it's important for us to faith forward on our respective paths to fulfilling our calling. Similar to how Jesus instructed Peter to step out onto the water in faith, He wants you to do the same. But when you do step out on faith, make sure that you are not chasing rainbows to get to the pot of gold. Instead strive to work towards the one goal of the kingdom, which is to tell everyone about God, and live as a reflection of Him.

Pause & Breathe Deeply

Part 2

Truth.

So, here we are chasing rainbows, but this time it's different. We are securing the bag inside the will of God. But I have to be honest. The truth is, we can learn the spiritual aspects of business, get some ah-mazing motivational quotes, repeat daily affirmations to ourselves to improve our mindset, and still not know what to do next to develop the business God has placed on the inside of us. You still feel stuck and confused as to what to do next? You need more practicality as to how to move forward. You need a plan and a roadmap. To be honest, even some early 2000's printed MapQuest instructions will work just fine as long as they tell you how to get from ideation to an actual business that's generating revenue.

As faith-based entrepreneurs, God instructed us to use wisdom. I interpreted that as we have to use the intellectual part of our minds to do what He wants us to do and be obedient to what he has called us to do. With that being said, I believe that there are times when we need to fast and pray over our businesses, and then there are times we need to work and apply wisdom. I have recognized that sometimes the lines are blurred, and folks will put in the work spiritually but not practically/physically. This is why many have faith but no works. I believe this is why God has begun to choose the hidden gems to rise and bring forth change.

I have dedicated this part of the book to giving you practical business knowledge. The knowledge that you can take and implement today for business. In this part of the book, I am covering what I believe to be some of the most important aspects to become a Priceless CEO of the business(es) God has called you to. *God says,*

"Blessed are those who find wisdom,
those who gain understanding."

Proverbs 3:13 NIV

Resolution.

There's nothing as motivating as a New Year. Every time January 1st rolls around, there's always a buzz in the air as we all collectively resolve to make positive changes in our lives. Whether it's becoming a better person, learning something new, or getting fit and healthy, we're filled with enthusiasm for these fresh resolutions. As an entrepreneur, you'll find out that you're not just making these New Year resolutions for your life; you're setting them for your business as well. While I am extremely supportive of this attitude, I also think it's time to be honest about resolutions; they seldom work. I don't want to be demotivating, but there are numerous reasons why setting resolutions will never work. Instead, it's time to think about setting goals for our businesses.

Breaking resolutions has practically become part of the calendar: set them on January 1st, break them by January 31st. This can be a demotivating situation to end up when it's personal. When it's for your business, it could be actively damaging. The issue is that resolutions tend to be very all or nothing. They represent a decision to do something or not do something, but they tell you nothing about how to achieve that.

For example, if your resolution is to double your clients in the new year, you're setting yourself up to fail if you've been in business less than a year. Yes, God is capable of anything. But the reality from wisdom is that it's a huge and admirable goal, but any setbacks will feel twice as crushing. It's too major of a change to happen in a year, but when many have it as a resolution, they believe it will automatically happen. Which brings us to another problem with new year resolutions. They're often impulsively made with no thought or planning on how to achieve them. This is why we need Godly wisdom.

As we all know by now, having a destination in mind is important, but it means nothing unless you know the way you're going to take.

I find that goals are considerably more attainable than resolutions even by definition alone. A goal is a clearly defined desired outcome with stages along the way. Turning our inspiring business ideas into resolutions is one thing, but turning them into tangible goals is considerably more important. Unlike resolutions, goals don't assume a complete about-turn overnight, which makes you more likely to succeed in your aims. Resolutions expect a drastic change, and this is hard enough when it's about your behaviors. But how can a business be expected to completely switch directions? It's not only unrealistic, but it's also often unnecessary.

Goal setting is a lot more like planning. You have to think about each stage along the way and what actions you need to take to achieve these milestones. Goals are also more flexible than resolutions. They provide you with a direction to travel in, but they also accept that you will take detours and need to reevaluate while you're on the journey. Setting new goals for your business is actually an exciting process and the best option for success. Imagine one year in the future and think about what you want your business to have achieved. Be honest with yourself about what is realistic, of course, but also push yourself out of your comfort zone.

It's a delicate balance with making sure you're not just creating new resolutions. But with practice, you'll get there! Make sure you write these goals down as a sure-fire way to increase your chances of success and focus your mind. If you work with a team, share your new goals with them to create a clear and powerful vision for the business.

God wants us to have visions and goals. He wants us to have resolutions. But neglecting the will of God can be the quickest way to get God to remove his hand from our lives. So as you create your resolutions, your goals, and your visions, think about what it is that God wants from your life. Are your resolutions aligned with what He wants?

Connecting this to the Word

Then the Lord replied:
"Write down the revelation and make it
plain on tablets so that a herald may run with it."

Habakkuk 2:2 NIV

Don't know about you,
but God promised
somethang!

Plan.

Often, entrepreneurship is indeed more of a mentality than action. However, the economic downturn has made it hard for some to get off the ground. However, many are increasingly turning away from traditional work towards being their boss. Remember, this doesn't have to mean heading up the new Facebook, but it could be effectively running a local coffee shop or a small construction company. No matter the size of the company, a business plan is an essential component. I also know that the thought of a business plan might scare you. But there are traditional business plans and strategic business plans. Most times, it's the traditional business plans that scare individuals from ever creating a plan. However, these two types of business plans serve very different purposes.

A traditional business plan is a document that outlines your company's structural framework and objectives (as well as the company's mission, vision, and value). It contains data for your competitors, in addition to financial and marketing plans. In general, a traditional business plan is created for new businesses that are looking for an investor. This plan is not often updated, if at all.

A strategic business plan is a document that contains not only the key objectives of the company (as well as the company's mission, vision, and value), it focuses more so on just the income opportunities for the company, product development, and services in which the business will grow. It focuses on strategically creating income streams and diversifying financial opportunities for the company's growth. The key elements of this plan help the owner know how to get from A to B with the company's operations to fulfill the company's vision. Ideally, a strategic business plan will help you focus on your business growth, as well as direction. This is updated frequently and is for your use.

Without a plan, you'll be missing out on all the long-term benefits, which have a strong foundation to your small business, and that's far more important than a few networking events near the beginning. Also, without a plan, you won't have clear objectives and a detailed map for your business. A business plan does not limit your innovation and ability to make changes. You have to see your business plans as a process, not instructions set in stone.

It's the springboard for starting your business, but it will evolve and change as the business does. Much like with any big commitment, small business planning needs to be given space sometimes and support from others.

Sometimes, your business plan might even need to be indulged a bit as you navigate this brave new world of small business ownership. As long as you see it as a guide to help you, not strict rules, you'll be just fine. To develop your plan, you need to do some pre-work.

While many just jump to creating a social media page,
I recommend doing your homework.

Research, have a cup of coffee, research some more. Become an expert on your product (of course!), the industry, and the market. When you look at corporate companies who are in the same industries, you will notice that they are constantly doing their research and innovating to show how they are doing it better. It's business, and as faith-based entrepreneurs, we should adopt some of these principles.

Next, you want to figure out what your goals are?
...well, besides making money, what is it?

Remember, you can't get anywhere if you don't know where you're going. Determining your goals will be what gives you focus as you develop your business and helps you start to lay out a roadmap to the future. Avoid anything vague or unachievable, like to become the most popular online marketing service; that isn't going to get you anywhere or tell your investors anything. Write down profit goals, market share goals, and if relevant, describe your vision; this gives you specific numbers to aim for.

Then you want to craft your business mission so you can have something to refer to for business decision making.

If setting out objectives is what gives you focus to move forward, crafting the business purpose is what will provide you guidance when you need to make decisions. It's about getting to the core of why your business exists and should be something that both customers and employees can relate to. Remember, the purpose goes beyond numbers; it is a way of constantly reminding you, as the founder of the business, why you started up. Is it to fulfill a need in the target market? To help people? To inspire them? Whatever it is, make sure it's not just to you, but to your investors, customers, and partners too. Take a moment to do a quick internet search for some of your most favorite companies. Do they live up to this statement? Is everything they do reflected in their mission statement? If you answered yes to both questions, then these are perfect examples of business mission statements. (My favorite mission statements are that of Chick-fil-A and Amazon).

You also need to understand your audience well.

Whatever your business purpose is, it will most likely be centered on your target audience, so you must understand them as well as you know yourself (maybe even better!) As part of your research, you will examine the current market; which segments are you planning to pursue? Think about whether you're aiming for particular age groups, gender, locations, or lifestyles. After identifying your target demographic, list the key features, characteristics, and importantly, the needs of this group. Their needs will help you shape your business and clarify your unique selling point. Lastly, determine their challenges and how the business service or products you offer are their solutions.

To continue planning, you have to determine y our unique value proposition.

When doing business planning, you can't pretend that you don't have any competition. Instead, you need to focus on what makes you different from your competitors. Many refer to this as your *'it factor'*. Your value proposition doesn't have to be about lower costs; it could be about the added service benefits customers get from working with you or the advanced technology you use that makes your company the more efficient choice. Think about creative solutions to the question that's always in consumers' minds. The biggest ride-sharing companies were able to crush traditional taxi service by having a unique value proposition.

Your business plan should also clearly identify your marketing strategies, a possible exit strategy, and my favorite, your income streams with segmented multiple income streams. Remember in part one, we discussed what the Bible says about this. But let's not forget that our plans in business have to go before God. It doesn't matter what the experts say or even if you went to school for 10 years to study the subject matter. Our plans rely on His will.

We can have a perfectly organized income stream in our business; a five-star course and a well-designed ebook; but what if it's not pleasing to God? What if through what you created someone's life won't be saved? This is why it is important that we give ourselves the grace to pivot in business to meet God's will, and so He can bless us spiritually and financially. We also have to realize as faith-based business owners, our businesses are not solely for us. It is to have generational impact within our family and other families.

Connecting this to the Word

"The plans of the diligent lead to profit as
surely as haste leads to poverty."

Proverbs 21:5 NIV

"Suppose one of you wants to build a tower.
Won't you first sit down and estimate the cost
to see if you have enough money to complete it?"

Luke 14:28 NIV

Diversify.

Diversification in business is something that a lot of small business owners do not speak often about. However, the very successful ones will tell you that they have found that diversifying their portfolio of services or products has been essential to their success in business. So, what is diversification anyways? By its definition, diversification means that you are reducing the risk associated with your business by adding services and products that will help your company's bottom line.

It's similar to creating income streams and is commonly confused due to the blurred lines of definition. But with diversification, you primarily focus on expanding through location, markets, and even customer base. To explain this in a simpler way, let's take a music artist for example. We know they make their money from music downloads, concerts, merchandise, and maybe events. But those various income streams are focused on one particular market and customer base. However, if that same music artist was to open a restaurant, own rental properties, or a cleaning company, that is called diversification. As each venture is focused on a different location, market, and customer base.

Another example may be a consultant who may have different customer bases by servicing newbie entrepreneurs and also corporate companies. Or a hair company that may offer wholesale and retail vending opportunities in multiple states or countries. This would allow them to tap into different locations and markets. The lines can sometimes get blurred between income streams and diversification. However, both are needed. The Bible instructs that we should have several options as the world may change, **Ecclesiastes 11:2 NIV.**

In fact, have you ever heard of the term: One Trick Pony?
It's a term that is often used to refer to one person who has only
one special feature, talent, or area of expertise.

The same can often be said for small businesses that serve only one audience, offer a very limited number of products or services, and tend to think very singularly regarding their objectives for growing their business. They have no other business revenue source, and this prevents them from being able to pivot in business in case the financial market crashes.

You can diversify in your business or outside of your business. Let's look at a big company selling computers.

They may also branch off to selling phones, and then later into a television streaming service. Each of these services targets a different segment of consumers. I know that you may not have a big company to diversify through serving different client types.

But a great way to diversify in your small business is by investing back into your business. This will allow you to expand your services or product listings. Using expansion as a diversification strategy will not only help your business move along more quickly, it will help you to determine how committed your audience is to some of your other services or products. This an important concept to consider because as your business ages, so does your customer base.

Overall, by offering a more diverse and well-rounded lineup of products and services, you will take your customers and clients along a journey that ensures they remain a part of your loyal followers in years to come. One key takeaway here is to spend some time researching the products and services you are planning on adding to your lineup. This is where many small business owners get it wrong, and you should make a decision that is based on facts or data, rather than current business trends which may be unsustainable.

God does not want us to struggle financially. However, I have come to realize that Christianity sometimes chastises wealth. Yet the word of God gives us specific instructions on how to gain wealth, alongside setting boundaries so that we are humble, not greedy, cheerful givers, and that we tithe. Our delay to follow some of these basic principles have caused us to be unable to do more work to glorify the kingdom. For example, how can you build the Christian school for children to learn while studying the word of God if you don't have access to finances?

Connecting this to the Word

"Invest in seven ventures, yes, in eight; you do not know what disaster may come upon the land."

Ecclesiastes 11:2 NIV

"Sow your seed in the morning, and at evening, let your hands not be idle, for you do not know which will succeed, whether this or that, or whether both will do equally well."

Ecclesiastes 11:6 NIV

Putting in this werk for God's blessings!

Quarterly.

Properly executing quarterly business plans is imperative in every business. To go into a new business quarter with goals of making $25,000 but no plan on how that $25,000 will be attained, is not a money-making strategy. Ideally, you have no plan for your upcoming business quarter. As an entrepreneur or business owner, you have to recognize that your quarterly business plans are a direct reflection of how much you want to make within the next three months. If you want to make $25,000, then some of the questions you should be asking yourself to develop your plan are:

What areas of your business will you focus on each month within that quarter?

What collaborations will you participate in?

What events will you host?

What items will you be selling each month?

How will you sell it?

Asking yourself these questions will help you to develop actionable steps that will contribute to your financial goals. These questions will also aid you in laying out your quarterly business plans on the table before the quarter begins. Besides these questions, there are a few other things needed to make your quarterly business plans priceless.

Review your previous quarter: If you are a current entrepreneur or business owner planning for the upcoming business quarter, it is almost imperative that you review your business strategies, systems, and structure of the previous quarter. You have to determine what worked for you in the previous quarter that you can keep and what did not that you should no longer have as a strategy. You have to take a moment and review your previous business quarter in its entirety to determine how you will develop your new plan for the upcoming quarter.

Set a goal: It is always lovely to set goals and you certainly need them to motivate you. However, setting quarterly goals will help you to have a clear picture of how you want to develop your quarterly business plan. These goals will not magically achieve themselves. You have to put in the work to execute your quarterly plans. Make them actionable. Setting the goal is one part, but creating actionable steps to achieve it is the actuality of how you achieve quarterly goals. When building your quarterly business plans, aim to have it focused on how you will achieve specific goals over the next few months.

Review your products and services: Review your products and services that you will be focused on selling over the next few months. Do they align with your mission, vision, and values? Are they going to confuse your consumers? For example,

Will you be selling shirts at a high-end price but the quality does not match?

How does the cost align with your business values?

How does selling shirts even align with your business mission to design websites?

What does selling shirts have to do with a webinar?

Create Personal Deadlines: It is important to create personal deadlines when making any plans for the business. Having personal deadlines will help you to create a time frame in which you have to execute portions of your plan.

For example, if you will have a webinar on April 25th, create a personal deadline to have the registration page completed and copies for emails drafted on April 10th. That way you are working on self-made deadlines that hold you responsible for executing your quarterly plan. This will also prevent you from having a plan that just sits there and gathers dust. Instead, you will now have a plan with an end date in sight. This will also allow you to implement specific actionable tasks every day that will let you meet up with that personal business deadline. This right here is a win-win.

Put the plan on paper: Putting the plan on paper is probably one of the simplest, but yet often forgotten aspect of quarterly planning. So, why is this important? Well, getting all of your business ideas, strategies, and goals out of your head and on paper will help you to not forget anything. This is as simple as going to the dollar store, picking up a notebook, and writing down your plans. Putting the plan on paper also helps you to have something to review for the next quarter. In general, this creates the documentation that you can always go back to reference. It also helps you to keep track of what worked and what did not work in the business. Lastly, you will know how much effort is needed to put into what did not work and what improvements are needed to be made next time.

Quarterly planning goes back to the concept of faith without works is dead. If you are clear on the path that God wants you to take in your life to live in your purpose, you also have to be clear on the details of how you will get there. That can only come through quarterly planning. It's not enough to have faith, you also have to have a plan.

Connecting this to the Word

"Put your outdoor work in order and get your fields ready;
after that, build your house."

Proverbs 24:27 NI*V*

Mindset.

CEOs must have the strength and drive to be able to handle everything that comes across their desk. If God gave it to you, it is because He knew you could handle it. Thinking, acting, and leading others as a CEO is very important if you are seeking the next level of success for your business. In order to achieve the results you are looking for, you MUST shift your mindset and think of yourself as a visionary! Start focusing on changing the way you think and stop handling the day to day running of your business as ordinary.

Focus on the bigger picture and envision what lies ahead in terms of growth. It's these small changes that can change your CEO mindset. Stop asking yourself, "What should I be doing or thinking right now?" But instead, ask yourself, "How can my team implement my visions?" Be prepared to take control of the reigns and take the blame as part of your leadership responsibilities as a CEO.

The best place to start is by strategizing a plan and creating a vision of where you would like your business to be in six months to a year from now. Create a list of every task and project that you have been working on every day. Can these be automated to run with little to no management? Start creating short videos of your tasks and projects, where you explain your expectations. Include how your future team can complete each task to their best ability while keeping the brand at the forefront. Taking action steps like this will help to shift your mindset into the CEO God has ordained you to be.

This will also aid in an easy transition when new team members come on board. As your team grows and tasks get redelegated, the last team member who was in charge of that particular task will now be in charge of training their replacement. This helps to transfer the responsibilities to someone other than yourself. In the end, you will be breaking free of the solopreneur and "I can do it all by myself" mindset. When transitioning from solopreneur to CEO mindset, there is a shift in how you do things.

Learning to get help and focus on your expertise is also a part of the CEO mindset. While many small business owners may consider it cost-effective to DIY their business, there will come a time when the day-to-day operation of their business will need the services of a true leadership team. Consider dedicating your company's complex daily operations to a Chief Operations Officer (COO) or have a Chief Financial Officer (CFO) create a budget and financial strategies aimed at growing your enterprise.

Jesus had 12 disciples as His team. All called to do something different. So why do you think you can do it all by yourself? God doesn't expect you to either, but you must have faith and put in the work, so He can bless you to bless others with employment.

Shifting into the CEO mindset also means reinvesting your profits back into your company's growth. Make sound investments in your business. Steer clear of spending frivolously and purge your current system of any unnecessary costs. Create operation budgets, and have a bookkeeper and an accountant to ensure your taxes are paid (Remember the law of the land).

The CEO mindset is how you will be able to increase your revenue so you can create jobs and opportunities for others. It is how you will be able to sow into the lives of others, and also take your family out of generational poverty. It is also how you will even treat yourself to that vacation in Greece! The CEO mindset is bigger than you, as you have to remember that someone may be praying for a boss like you. When I realized I needed to fully step into my CEO role, it scared me. I questioned why it would be me and was I even really capable. But after I fully accepted my calling, I soon realized that God would never leave me stranded in fulfilling my purpose.

Connecting this to the Word

"Those who live according to the flesh have their minds set on what the flesh desires; but those who live in accordance with the Spirit have their minds set on what the Spirit desires.

Romans 8:5 NIV

Not right now, anxiety.
I'm busy handling
things for God!

Mental.

Becoming an entrepreneur is a dream of many – you're working to make your dreams come true, and there's a scope to be creative, independent, and self-sufficient. Many of us have worked hard to get to this point and are justifiably proud of our achievements. What's more? We project an image of resilience in the face of challenges. After all, we think, should we really be running our own business if we can't cope with tough times? But behind the inspirational hashtags and success stories, there's a darker story: the fact that up to 70% of entrepreneurs suffer from depression or a form of mental disorder.

So now is the time to take a close look at mental health and entrepreneurship. It's important to shed light and be a voice in mental health awareness, rather than a hindrance. So why is there such a close link between entrepreneurship and mental disorders? There are multiple interlinking reasons, but let's start with the most obvious one: stress (no spoilers here!). Yes, other jobs are stressful too, but when you're an entrepreneur, it feels like you're always on. Work seeps into all parts of our lives, so it feels like you never get a break, and without robust self-care strategies and boundaries, it can feel impossible to escape that stress.

Compounding to this is the fact that the successes and failures of your company are so fused with your identity, so you feel them deeply. There's also the emotional labor of putting on a good front. There can be (often internal) pressure to always appear to 'have it all together' so that clients and potential investors view you as flawless. There's still a stigma attached to mental health, and the fear that stakeholders might be 'put off' by 'weakness' is toxic. The successes and failures of your company are so fused with your identity, so you feel them deeply.

This is one of the many reasons why entrepreneurs are so susceptible to mental health illnesses. Finally, there's the fact that while coping with these pressures, we are often isolated. Entrepreneurship is, at least initially, a solitary path. Social interactions tend to be networking situations, where we're worrying about making a good impression – there's that emotional labor again. Suddenly, that 70% statistic doesn't seem so surprising, right? Don't worry, it's not all bad news.

In my business, I have learned to utilize business planning techniques to avoid stress and burnout. I implement the things I do in phases. I seek help when needed and have mastered the art of saying no to avoid feeling overwhelmed. It wasn't always that way for me, but after having a few embarrassing anxiety attacks, I've learned. After observing other individuals being admitted to the hospital for stress or even mental institutions from stress, I've learned.

On an individual basis, you can also do a lot to ensure you avoid stress and burnout, common problems in entrepreneurship. Your company is your baby, something you pour your heart and soul into, so it can be hard to step away, even when it's vital for your mental health. Just remember that you'll do better work when you are healthy, happy, and have a good work-life balance (whatever that means to you!). We're all confident in using effective planning techniques for our business, setting long-term objectives, breaking them down into more manageable goals, putting things down on paper, and scheduling our working days, so why not utilize these to help you avoid burnout?

Being strategic and organized with your time is one of the best ways to manage your stress. Working flat-out to the point of exhaustion isn't good for you or your company. Making sure that the goals you are setting are manageable and ambitious is great, but not if it's unrealistic. Set milestones along the way, and reward yourself for your achievements. Establish routines to stop time from being wasted. Procrastination and anxiety go hand in hand, so it's important to stick to a schedule to avoid both of these! When planning your time, make sure you schedule in time for self-care as well. That might be exercise, phone-free time, baking, cocktails with friends; whatever counts as self-care for you, don't abandon it.

Activating all your business planning techniques means that your processes will flow much more smoothly. In that way, there will be far fewer moments of panic and stress. When you've got a lot of work, it can be easy to fall into a trap of thinking you don't have time to plan, but committing to this saves you time in the long run. It also saves you from tangled projects and missed deadlines in the future. Entrepreneurship can be a joy and there's no reason to be ashamed if you sometimes struggle mentally.

Connecting this to the Word

*"Cast your cares on the Lord and he will sustain you;
he will never let the righteous be shaken."*

Psalms 55:22 NIV

Balance.

Oh yea, balance. That elusive spirit that we are all chasing. Balance is the dream, the goal, the ultimate sign that we have managed our lives and work successfully so that we lead a well-adjusted and stress-minimal life. I'd say stress-free, but that's an illusion! In today's world of work apps, social networks, and constant connection, the work-life balance might seem like an illusion as we can never indeed switch off. There have been countless articles proclaiming the death of balance, and apparently, we now have to accept that there is no such thing. I'm not ready to give up yet. However, implementing consistent work-life balance strategies means that you too can achieve that Holy Grail.

One of the main things that makes the unicorn of work-life balance seem so elusive is that no one knows what it is. The common perception seems to be that it is in a work zone from 9 am to 5 pm (or some combination of eight hours) and then being able to shake off the workday and enjoy some downtime without work interruptions. The fact of the matter is, this just isn't going to happen. With the prevalence of technology in our working lives, switching off isn't as simple as going home and forgetting about it. This is even truer for entrepreneurs, who feel a tremendous sense of ownership over what's happening at work. It's hard when you've got so many balls juggling in the air to feel like you're ever going to be able to compartmentalize. Work is a huge part of many of our lives, and getting away from that often can't be achieved.

Work-life balance is entirely achievable with a little bit of effort. It takes practice, patience, and persistence!

Even in my world of "mastering" time management, I still sometimes find myself in positions where I have to make quick decisions about resolutions and work-life balance. Sometimes I will say I am going to leave on time, go to the gym, and cook a healthy dinner. Then there's last-minute feedback from a client, then all my deadlines will get pulled forward, and I end up working until midnight. At times like this, work-life balance never seems further away. Despite all this, I still believe that work-life balance is entirely achievable with a little bit of effort. So how do we catch this constantly shifting sprite? Mostly, you have to be strict with yourself (which is the hardest type of tough to be!) and consistently implement work-life balance strategies. What strategies are important?

First is, of course, DISCONNECT. Listen up, entrepreneurs! You might have heard it before, but it's vital. That phone lighting up is always going to lasso you back into work even when you're chilling on the sofa with Netflix, so you need to turn it off and put it somewhere else. Also, if it's only for an hour a day, that disconnected hour will provide you with so much balance. I have digital well-being apps on my phone that blocks out social media for certain times of the day. I also have timers on each app with an allocated time I'm allowed to be on each day.

Secondly, it is all about PREPARATION. It will come as no surprise that I am a prominent advocate of careful planning. When you feel submerged in work, it's hard to make time for schedules and to-do lists, but it's time worth spending. Mapping out your week ahead of time is going to give you a much better idea of the time you have. And it's not just about planning your work, it's also about your personal life. It might seem strange to schedule time with family and friends, but it means you'll commit to it much more. It's hard when you're running your business because it means so much to you, but you need to prioritize self-care, whatever that looks like to you, as much as you prioritize work deadlines. Whether it's exercise, a long bubble bath, or a cocktail or two, taking time for yourself is a guaranteed way to prevent overload and help you refocus. For me, I take the weekends and holidays off. I also allocate vacation time for myself in my business.

Finally, and most importantly, take VACATIONS. It's easy for business owners to see holidays as extra time to focus on those projects that need to get finished, but holidays and vacations are supposed to act as breathing spaces in your year. Working through them means you never reset and all your days blend into one. Relentless work is not the way to achieve either balance or a successful business, so give yourself a break! When I'm on vacation away from my business, nothing gets done from my end. If my team can't handle it, then it just has to stay. There are autoresponders and systems in place. Each client is checked on prior to me checking out. Lastly, I jokingly remind myself that if it's going to virtually burn down when I'm away, then I'll deal with it when I get back.

What you'll notice about my work-life balance strategies is that none of them suggest setting rigid work hours or not responding to emails after traditional working hours. After all, this might not represent a balance to you. If you're on edge sitting at home thinking of all the things you need to do for upcoming projects, that's not going to do much for your well-being. So, sometimes you might as well be at work, or perhaps you need to hire someone for a few hours so you can stop thinking. Then again, the reality is that many of us are living different lifestyles and may need to respond to emails after the traditional working hours. Making work-life balance achievable has a lot to do with accepting that balance is not necessarily a 50-50 split and that it is a fluid situation.

Some weeks, your priorities might be more focused around work;
some weeks, it is more concentrated on exciting events in your
personal life.

What's important is to not sacrifice your life for your business, and to remember that you can achieve a harmony that aligns with your values in life. Being clear on your values helps you to be clear on your boundaries at different points in time. Boundaries are the keyword here. You have to accept that the traditional idea of work-life balance is a bit of an illusion that you often can't control or perhaps don't want to if it's your business at stake. What you can manage are your boundaries. Remember, what work-life balance looks like to you is a personal choice, and as long as you feel rewarded and present in everything you do, you're guaranteed to stay productive and happy. But even God rested on the 7th day.

Connecting this to the Word

"And on the seventh day, God ended his work which he had made; and he rested on the seventh day from all his work which he had made."

Genesis 2:2 KJV

I can't afford to mess up
what God is doing!

Avoid.

There's a lot to cover when it comes to business. While I couldn't cover it all in this book, I hope that this foundational advice will assist you on your journey as a faith-based entrepreneur. But knowing that there is still so much more for you to learn, I will also help you understand what you should avoid to successfully manage the ministry that God has given you.

Skipping the business basics: Modern solopreneurs and small businesses tend to skip the business basics. These foundational steps are sometimes overshadowed by the power of social media. In other words, most believe that social media is a foundational step in business when in reality it is not. The best businesses start with a business plan which consists of goals, strategies, business models, and much more. These foundational steps are a vital process, as they help to navigate the success of a business.

Having no other plan: Having no other plan besides the business plan is also another common mistake. Other plans are also important, including quarterly plans, annual plans, marketing plans, and even product launch plans. This mistake is commonly made because many ignore the fact that entrepreneurship is a series of rational choices. In other words, to be successful at entrepreneurship, you will need to be strategic.

Not executing the plan: Not executing the plan tends to happen because of fear or lack of effort. The fear of having a failed plan or project causes many to stop at the thought of the implementation process. If this is you, then you should realize that failure will happen in entrepreneurship, but it is what you do afterward that will matter the most. Therefore, it is best to just execute the plan. Then some realize the amount of work they have to do, so they simply do not put in the work. If this is you, then you should realize that plans cannot execute themselves; therefore, it is best to just execute the plan. Overall, you have to realize that souls are counting on you. So the longer you stay stagnant is the longer souls stay stuck.

Being blinded by social media: We will not deny that there is power in social media. It is most certainly needed for any modern business owner. However, individuals frequently forget that business is more than this. They negate important aspects such as collaborations, networking, and other joint venture partnerships. They also forget that the goal of social media for businesses is not just to get followers or likes, they forget about business policies, standard operating procedures, employee handbooks, contracts, accounting and so much more. The focal point of this mistake is to not spend so much time on social media that you forget to work on organizing the internal operations of your business. Without proper structures in place for your business, you will become an overwhelmed and overworked business owner.

Lack of organizational structure: Once a business hits the six-figure mark or has a significant increase in client workload, then it is time to develop organizational structure. Organizational structures help businesses to establish different units for the goals in which the business wants to accomplish. These structures do not have to be for large corporations only, but it can also be used in small businesses. Lack of organizational structure is a mistake that small businesses tend to make because they get scared when they hear the term. However, your goal here is to look for a way to structure your company that will ease off some of the burdens from the CEO and avert their feeling of being overwhelmed.

Believing you can do it all alone: Entrepreneurship cannot be a successful journey alone. Believing you can do it all alone will cause your business to suffer many consequences, including unsatisfied consumers, missing revenue, and stagnating growth. While many are scared to grow their business with a team, it is needed as a CEO to keep your sanity. Implementing strong team-building strategies is a great start to getting over the belief that you can do it alone. A strong team includes experts who are genius in what they do, passionate, have the desire to build with you and not against you, professional, take initiative, generate new ideas, and most importantly, they understand the role of their jobs and love their compensation package.

Failing to lead your team: Failing to lead your team can affect your business and cause you to miss your business goals. Leadership skills come naturally to others and some may need to receive leadership training. An important aspect of leading a team is creating job descriptions, implementing team-building activities, setting boundaries, and having standards for evaluations. Leadership for your team is as important as the captain of a ship. Without the captain's leadership, where will the ship go? Simply put, failing to lead your team will cause your ship to sink.

Setting unrealistic financial goals: It is so important that we make our plans realistic. You can plan to make 100k. But is that a realistic plan based on your industry or product type? Is it realistic if you do not even have an audience yet? Creating the plan is one thing, but making it realistic is necessary. Solopreneurs and small businesses should tune out what others are saying about their business finances and focus on the reality of their businesses when setting their goals.

Lack of honesty: Honesty is the best policy, and this is something that solopreneurs and small businesses should stick with. While it can be hard to be patient and wait for business success, it is better than being untruthful. For example, some individuals are untruthful with their profit margins, or how they acquire social media followers, and then call themselves social media gurus or builders of a millionaire lifestyle. This is an obvious lack of honesty in business that will catch up with you in the long run. Your business supporters will love you more when you are honest.

As you continue along your business journey, you will find things that you need to avoid. Give yourself grace to grow and ask God for wisdom of what you should be doing each and every step of the way.

Connecting to the Word

"Know also that wisdom is like honey for you:
If you find it, there is a future hope for you,
and your hope will not be cut off."

Proverbs 24:14 NIV

Souvenirs.

You ever gave your parents a macaroni necklace as a kid in school? Or a clay bowl? Or what about the fingerprint painting? Or perhaps what you gave them is a picture to place on their favorite table. Like maybe one of your school graduation pictures? Or your wedding? Almost every parent keeps something from their child as souvenirs. Especially when they are proud of their work.

So what about our heavenly Father? God. Have you made Him proud? What souvenirs do you think He will be proud of and want to put in His mansion? I hope that God is proud of how I answered my calling in business. When He returns, He should say well-done Sidjae, you didn't chase the rainbows in search of the pot of gold. And even if you did chase the rainbows you made sure I was by your side and that is why I gave you the desires of your heart.

Connecting this to the Word

"His master replied,
'Well done, good and faithful servant! You
have been faithful with a few things;
I will put you in charge of many things.
Come and share your master's happiness!'

Matthew 25:23

Conclusion.

Chasing Rainbows is something we all do once we embark on the entrepreneurship journey. We begin this crazy race with a lot of monetary goals at the forefront. We are securing the bag, or in some cases, bags. Our focus to ensure that we have control and power over our finances often leads to us excluding God from our business. Or we may even create a business that he never placed his will for our life. And being the silly children of God that we are, here come the tears and tantrums. We are left with our tears begging and pleading with God to bless our plans. Crying out to Him in the latter when we should have first involved Him in our plans.

We cannot just be spiritually built for business but should also be using the wisdom and resources God placed within others to further our endeavors. We should ignore trends and realize when we are not called to business in its entirety, or a particular business, and may be operating outside the will of God because of our desires to pursue the bag. As faith-based entrepreneurs, we have to remember that only what we do for Christ will last. Only what we build with his divine hand in it will be sustainable. This journey is one that will require endurance and strength. This strength can only come from God.

This is why it is important to ensure that we are chasing rainbows and pursuing the bag inside the will of God. It makes the journey smoother and even sweeter as you realize that the work you are doing is benefiting His kingdom.

Ready to become a Priceless CEO?

Visit bit.ly/PricelessCEOMasterclass to join the next cohort of Dr.Price's *Priceless CEO Masterclass*.

Pursue The Bag

...inside the will of God.

www.ingramcontent.com/pod-product-compliance
Lightning Source LLC
Chambersburg PA
CBHW071932090426
42811CB00042B/2422/J